Pirates Carolinas for Kids

Terrance Zepke

Pineapple Press, Inc.
Sarasota, Florida

Inquiries should be addressed to:

Pineapple Press, Inc.
P.O. Box 3889
Sarasota, Florida 34230

www.pineapplepress.com

Library of Congress Cataloging-in-Publication Data

Zepke, Terrance
  Pirates of the Carolinas for kids / Terrance Zepke. -- 1st ed.
     p. cm.
  Includes bibliographical references and index.
  ISBN 978-1-56164-459-9 (pb : alk. paper)
  1. Pirates--North Carolina--Atlantic Coast--History--Juvenile literature. 2. Pirates--South Carolina--Atlantic Coast--History--Juvenile literature. 3. Pirates--North Carolina--Atlantic Coast--Biography--Juvenile literature. 4. Pirates--South Carolina--Atlantic Coast--Biography--Juvenile literature. 5. Atlantic Coast (N.C.)--History, Naval--Juvenile literature. 6. Atlantic Coast (S.C.)--History, Naval--Juvenile literature. 7. North Carolina--History--Colonial period, ca. 1600-1775--Juvenile literature. 8. South Carolina--History--Colonial period, ca. 1600-1775--Juvenile literature. I. Title.
  F262.A84Z47 2009
  910.4'5--dc22
                                                      2009019082

First Edition
10 9 8 7 6 5 4 3 2 1

Design by Shé Hicks
Printed in China

Contents

Part I

ALL ABOUT PIRACY   4

Early Piracy   5
Life of a Pirate   5
Pirate Truths and Myths   7
Pirate Ships   10
Pirate Weapons   11
Pirate Terms   12
Piracy Today   19

Part II

PIRATES OF THE CAROLINAS   20

Blackbeard   21
Anne Bonny   31
John "Calico Jack" Rackham   35
Mary Read   37
Henry "Long Ben" Avery   41
William "Billy" Lewis   43
Stede "the Gentleman Pirate" Bonnet   47
Charles Vane   51
William Kidd   55

Part III

MORE PIRATE STUFF   62

Pirate Quiz   63
Pirate Activities   65
Pirate Museums   66
Pirate Resources   67

Quiz Answers (but don't peek!)   68
Index   71

Part I

ALL ABOUT PIRACY

Early Piracy

Pirates have almost always been around. Records show that piracy dates back more than 2,500 years. Piracy was biggest during the late seventeenth and early eighteenth centuries. That was the Golden Age of Piracy.

This was a time when many European countries were at war with each other. Their governments let privateers attack enemy ships. Privateers were nothing more than pirates who had permission from their king or queen. Privateers shared what they got with their government. The government needed the money to pay for wars.

Queen Anne's War was the biggest war of that time. It was between England and France, and it lasted ten years. Thousands of men served in the British Royal Navy and as privateers. When the war was over in 1713, they were no longer needed. There were no jobs, so they became pirates.

A popular sailing route was from Europe to the Caribbean and back again. Merchant ships carried food, fine fabrics, rum, tobacco, gunpowder, coffee, gold, and many other valuable goods. Pirates also traveled this route to steal from the merchant ships.

Favorite places for pirates to weigh anchor included ports in Jamaica and Madagascar, as well as in Cuba, Hispaniola, and the Bahamas. The Bahamas were called New Providence back then. Pirates liked these places because there were not many laws. These islands welcomed pirates and their money.

Piracy has changed over the years. But pirates are still sailing the seas.

Life of a Pirate

Who were these men and women who chose to become sea robbers? Most pirates were poor men who were just trying to make a living. They did not have any education or job skills. A few of the famous pirates, like Captain Kidd and Anne Bonny, had other reasons. Stede Bonnet and Captain Kidd became pirates because they were bored with their lives. They wanted excitement. Anne Bonny chose piracy rather than marry a man her father had chosen for her. You'll find out more about them in the next section.

Pirates lived hard and fast. They spent what they got as fast as they got it. They did not save money because most pirates did not live to be old. They often died in battle. Sometimes they got caught and sent to prison—or they were hanged.

Sometimes they died from the harsh conditions on pirate ships. Pirate ships had big crews. Lots of men were needed to fight when they attacked merchant ships. There was not enough room for all of them to sleep at the same time. They had to take turns. Pirates got sick because they did not eat enough fruits and vegetables. This caused a disease called scurvy. There was not enough fresh water either. Battle wounds were often not properly treated.

So why would anyone want to be a pirate? Some men joined for adventure, but most had no choice. They had no skills to get a job. Some men were even tricked or forced to become pirates.

A pirate crew was led by a captain. He was elected by the crew. His job was to find treasure! The quartermaster was second in command and was also elected. The quartermaster had many important jobs. He gave each man his share of what they stole from other ships. He punished crew members when needed and was also in charge of prisoners. He let the captain know when the crew was unhappy about anything. Other officers on pirate ships were the boatswain, gunner, sailing master, first mate, surgeon, carpenter, musicians, and sailmakers.

Life at sea was usually exciting. Pirates chased merchant ships and were in battle often. They also partied and played. But life at sea could be boring at times. Pirates sometimes sat around with nothing to do. They

What did pirates eat?

Whatever they could get their hands on! They ate mostly soups or stews made with potatoes and fish. They had dry biscuits called "hardtack" at almost every meal. Treats were turtles, turtle eggs, hens, hen eggs, and wild pig.

had to wait for winds so they could sail. Or they had to wait for a merchant ship to come their way. Or they had to do chores. It could take weeks to clean the ship's hull or repair sails after a bad storm.

When they were not at sea, pirates spent many hours making ship repairs that could only be made when the ship was out of the water. This was called "careening." First the pirates had to find a spot on the beach that would be hard for others to find. This gave them the chance to do their work without getting caught by the authorities. Then the ship was run ashore at high tide, with one of the ship's sides in the air. That way the pirates could fix and clean the hull or other parts of the ship. Pirates also enjoyed the pleasures of life on land when they were no longer at sea. They went into port cities and spent their loot on food, drink, and whatever else they needed or wanted.

Maybe the best thing about being a pirate was that he could work when he wanted to. A pirate could spend months on shore having a good time in the Caribbean. Then when he got bored or ran out of money, he could join the next pirate ship.

Pirate Truths and Myths

There have been many things said about pirates over the years. Some are true. Some are not. Did pirates really have wooden legs? Did pirates really walk around with parrots on their shoulders? Did they really maroon mutinous pirates? Did anyone really walk the plank? Did pirates really bury their treasure? Let's explore these questions.

Did pirates have wooden legs? Yes! If a pirate lost a leg during battle, it was replaced with a wooden one. If a hand was lost during battle, it was replaced with a hook.

What about parrots? Yes, they were popular with pirates. Pirates kept them as pets during long voyages to entertain the crew. They were also sold at market for high prices.

Was there such a thing as marooning? Yes, pirates who tried to take over from the captain were marooned, or left behind, in a tiny rowboat or on a deserted island. Sometimes they were given a jug of water and a pistol with one bullet. Pirates liked to punish when necessary, but they did not like to kill one another. Marooning a fellow pirate or a prisoner was their

way of getting rid of someone without killing him. Survival was possible if the pirate got rescued from the deserted island or boat. Charles Vane is one example of a marooned pirate who survived.

Did pirates bury their treasure? Not very often. The only time a pirate would bury treasure was when he thought he was about to get caught. Then he might hide it and return as soon as possible for it. Captain Kidd buried his treasure so that he wouldn't be caught with it when he came back to America. He knew that the authorities would take it away from him. He didn't want that to happen because he wanted to use the treasure in exchange for his freedom.

Was walking the plank fact or fiction? This did happen, but it was rare. Instead, other pirates who needed to be punished were usually marooned in a rowboat. Prisoners didn't normally walk the plank either. They were more often thrown overboard into the sea to drown. Henry Avery threw some prisoners overboard when food supplies began to get low.

Pirate Ships

To win any war, two things are needed: a good plan of action and weapons. The most important weapon was the ship.

If a pirate knew he would be at sea attacking large merchant ships, he would use a large ship that had three masts. These three-masted ships were also called square-rigged ships. They were not as fast as smaller ships because they weighed more—up to 300 tons. But they held more crew and could carry up to forty cannons.

Smaller ships were used by pirates who were not far out at sea. These ships were made for speed. They were easier to move around in shallow water, such as the inlets and sounds of the Carolinas.

There were many different types of ships, but these were three of the most popular during the Golden Age of Piracy:

The *sloop* was the smallest. This ship weighed less than 100 tons. It was the fastest and was easy to use. A sloop could hold up to twelve cannons and fifty pirates. It was usually a single-mast ship, but it could have as many as two or three masts.

The most popular name for a ship at that time was *Adventure*. Pirates usually painted over the outside of their gun ports. This was done to hide them. They didn't want merchant ships to know they were pirates until it was too late!

The *schooner* weighed a little more than a sloop and had a different design. Since it was heavier, it was not as fast. It held up to eight cannons and seventy-five pirates. These ships had two to six masts. The two-masted schooner was the most common kind.

The *brigantine* was bigger than the sloop and the schooner. It weighed about 150 tons. This type of ship could carry one hundred pirates and twelve cannons. It usually had two masts.

Pirate Weapons

Boarding ax: This is like a regular ax but heavier. It was used to slash sails, cut through wood, smash skulls, and break down doors.

Cannons: There are many different sizes and types of cannons. Pirates used them to shoot bombs, nails, tacks, and musket balls. Gun holes in the ship were opened during battle so that the cannons could be fired.

Cutlass: A short, heavy sword that curves at the tip

cutlass

Dagger: A big knife with a thicker blade than the blade of a normal knife

Grappling irons: Metal hooks used to board an enemy ship

Grenade: A small explosive thrown onto an enemy ship before boarding

Guns or pistols: Seventeenth-century pistols and guns could fire off only one bullet before reloading. Most pirates had holsters that could hold as many as six guns.

Types of guns and rifles
Flintlock (popular pirate gun)
Musket (single-shot rifle)
Musketoon (sort of a mini-musket)
Blunderbuss (like a musketoon)

Powder horn: A pouch or box that held gunpowder

Soap or grease: This was used to make a deck slippery. If your enemy slid and fell as soon as his feet hit your deck, you had him!

Spears: Sharp-pointed sticks thrown from your ship at the enemy. This was done to injure as many enemies as possible before hand-to-hand combat.

Swivel guns: These were small cannons that could shoot a 70-pound ball up to half a mile. They could be moved around the deck to wherever they were needed. They were placed in a holder, which made them easier to aim and fire. A fast gunner could clean and reload a swivel or swing gun in under four minutes.

Tacks: These are like the ones used on a bulletin board. They were spread out on a ship's deck. When an enemy jumped aboard your ship, he would cut his feet! Most Caribbean sailors did not wear shoes, so they could really get hurt.

Pirate Terms
Learn these terms and you will be able to talk like a real pirate!

Aft: The rear of the ship

"Ahoy": "Hello"

Ballast: A ship stabilizer
(Anything heavy enough to weigh down the ship was used as the ballast. Water barrels or cargo were popular stabilizers.)

"Belay": "Be quiet"

Bilge: This word has two meanings. It can mean silly or foolish talk, but bilge is also what sailors called the lowest area of a ship. This is inside the hull along the keel. It fills up with bad-smelling water called bilge or bilge water.

"Blimey!": An exclamation of surprise

Blockade: To prevent or block a ship from reaching or leaving a port

Bow: The front part of a ship

Bowsprit: A spar at a ship's prow
(A spar is a long wooden pole that sticks out from the prow at the front of a sailing ship. It is important because it supports the sails.)

Brethren of the Coast: This is what pirates used to call themselves. They were a brotherhood. They had a Code of Conduct. The code was made up of basic rules that pirates were expected to follow.

Careen: This was when a ship was turned over on its side on land for repairs or cleaning. Barnacles and other sea creatures had to be scraped from the bottom of the ship.

Cargo: Cargo is the goods being transported on a merchant ship. Cargo could be anything from tobacco to gold. Pirates liked any kind of cargo. They could use it, sell it, or trade it for what they needed.

Pirates were also called buccaneers, sea robbers, sea rovers, marauders, filibusters, corsairs, freebooters, and sea dogs. Pirate treasure was also called a prize, loot, booty, and plunder.

Caulk: A mixture of oakum (rope fibers) and tar used to waterproof a wooden ship

Chantey or Shanty: Any sailor sea song

Chart: A map of the oceans and coastlines

Crow's nest: This was a small platform near the top of a mast. It was used as a lookout for enemy or merchant ships.

Davy Jones' locker: A nickname for the bottom of the ocean

"Dead men tell no tales": A pirate saying about why they don't like to leave witnesses

Doubloon: A Spanish gold coin

"Fair winds": Fond wishes for good luck at sea

Galleon: A large sailing ship that was common in the 1600s

Gibbet: This was a cage used to publicly display the bodies of pirates after they had been executed. Family or friends might steal the corpse if it was not locked inside a gibbet.

"Gangway": "Get out of the way"

"Godspeed": Another way of saying "Good-bye and good luck on your voyage"

Go on the account: To take up piracy

Grenade: A small, hand-thrown explosive used in battle

Grog: An alcoholic beverage, such as rum or ale

Grub: Slang for food

Fore: Front end of the ship

Flogging: A public whipping for crew members who did something wrong

Hands: Hands were workers on a ship. If someone yelled "Hands!" it meant "All hands on deck!"

"Handsomely": Means "Hurry up" or "Be quick about it"

Haven: A safe place to hide and make ship repairs or just to party

Hardtack: This was a biscuit served at most meals. It was hard and stale. There were often little bugs inside that had gotten into the flour. Before eating the hardtack, pirates had to tap it against the table to shake the bugs out!

Hijack: To hijack is to take a ship and cargo by force. Pirates today are often called hijackers, but they are still pirates.

Hull: The outer part or shell of a ship

Jolly Roger: A type of pirate flag

Keel: The keel is like the spine of the ship. It is a timber beam that runs across the bottom of a ship's hull.

Keelhaul: This was a terrible punishment. A person was dragged under the ship! The victim came close to drowning and suffered bad wounds.

Knot: A way to measure a ship's speed. One knot equals one nautical mile per hour. Knot is also is a way of tying ropes.

Landlubber: A non-sailor or someone who gets seasick

Letters of Marque: These were papers issued by a government during a war. A letter of marque gave permission for the privateer to attack enemy ships. The loot was split between the privateer, the crew, and his government. Privateers were nothing more than licensed pirates!

Logbook: A daily account of shipboard activities on a voyage

Maroon: This was a type of punishment for a pirate. He was left on a deserted island or in a small boat with little chance of survival or rescue.

Merchant ship: A trading ship that had cargo that pirates wanted

Nautical mile: A distance at sea that is a little longer than a mile on land

"No quarter": This meant that no mercy would be shown.

Piece of eight: This was a silver coin worth one Spanish peso. Sometimes it was divided into eight pieces.

Pillage: To raid, rob, or plunder

Pirate round: A round-trip voyage from North America or the Caribbean to West Africa and the Indian Ocean

Piragua: A dug-out canoe sometimes used by Caribbean pirates

Poop deck: This is the highest deck at the aft end of a large ship. There are no poop decks on smaller ships.

Port: The left side of the ship if facing toward the prow

Pound: The British form of money, used also in America before 1776. The symbol for this is £. Pirates' loot would have been measured in pounds instead of dollars.

Prahu: A fast little boat used by Asian pirates

Privateer: This was a pirate who had permission from a government to attack ships of countries with which they were at war. Privateers shared what they got with the government.

Prow: The nose of the ship, the part of the bow above the waterline

Quarterdeck: The aft part of the upper deck of a smaller ship

Quartermaster: This officer was second in command, after the captain, on a ship. He was the voice of the crew. If the crew was unhappy about something, the quartermaster was the one who told the captain.

Rig: The masts and sails of a ship

Rigging: The rope system for masts and sails of a ship

Rudder: A moveable board at the back of a ship that controls its steering

Sailcloth: A heavy canvas used for making the sails

"Sail ho": What the lookout or any crew member says when he has spotted a ship or the sail of a ship

Scuppers: These are openings along the edges of a ship's deck. They are there so that water will go into the sea instead of collecting on the deck.

Scurvy: This is a disease caused by lack of Vitamin C. Most pirates had poor diets and did not eat enough fruit, which is full of Vitamin C.

Seaworthy: Said of a boat or ship that was safe for a voyage at sea

Shipshape: This means everything looks good and all is well on board.

"Shiver me timbers": An expression of surprise or fear

"Splice the mainbrace": Another way of saying "Let's enjoy a cold drink"

Spyglass: A small telescope

Starboard: The right side of a ship when facing toward the prow

Tavern or Pub: This was a place that served food and drink. It was popular with pirates.

Watch: A time when someone was assigned to stand guard or be the lookout

Weigh anchor: To bring the anchor up to set sail

Piracy Today

Piracy is not over. It will always be around. It has changed over the years, though. Pirates now use high-speed boats. They used to attack merchant ships. Now they attack freighters, cruise ships, ocean liners, and private boats. Freighters are modern-day merchant ships loaded with cargo crates.

What do pirates get these days? The loot can be anything. It is often jewelry, electronics, boat parts, or cash. Sometimes the pirates don't take anything. They ask for money for the safe return of the boat, crew, and passengers. This is called a ransom.

The problem is serious. The International Maritime Bureau was set up to help deal with crimes that take place on the ocean, including piracy. Piracy is really widespread in Asia, the Java Sea, and the South China Sea.

The number of reported pirate attacks has risen in recent years. There were probably lots more that were not even reported. Freighter owners often do not report pirate attacks because they do not want the people they do business with to find out. Those companies might think their cargo is not safe. Pirates are bad for business!

Modern-day pirates are very dangerous. They are armed with powerful weapons. Blackbeard liked to throw small grenades onto an enemy ship. Today, pirates can use rocket-propelled grenades.

What is being done about this? New technology is being used. The Inventus UAV is a vehicle that flies without a pilot. It has cameras that show a captain if there is a pirate ship hiding nearby. If there is one, the captain can stay away from that place or let the authorities know.

The Secure-Ship system is another way to stop pirates. It is an electric "fence" that goes around the ship so pirates cannot board. A pirate will get a 9,000-volt shock if he tries to climb over it! The minute a pirate touches it, a loud alarm goes off and bright lights come on.

These are expensive, so not all ships have them. Most do have a good tracking device. Big ships must have a tracking device aboard. The tracking device lets the ship's owner or the authorities know where the ship is at all times. If the ship is taken over by pirates, the tracking device sends a secret message to law enforcement officials.

Part II

PIRATES OF THE CAROLINAS

BLACKBEARD

Blackbeard's real name was Edward Teach or Thatch. He had an exciting life. This sea robber captured fifty ships while he was a pirate. He led four hundred men at the peak of his career.

He was probably born in Bristol, England, in either 1675 or 1690. What year he was born in and whether his name is Teach or Thatch depends on which historical records you believe. As a boy he loved the sea. He could not stay away from the harbor. Every day he watched the ships come and go. Every night he dreamed about life at sea.

His dream came true. He became a privateer during Queen Anne's War (1702–1713). A privateer was like a pirate. The only difference was that a privateer got a sheet of paper that was signed by the king or queen. The paper was called a commission. The commission said that a privateer could attack enemy ships. Cargo from these ships could be taken. It was used to pay for wars, like Queen Anne's War. This was legal because the king or queen said it was all right. Many privateers became pirates when there was no war.

By 1716, Teach met up with pirate Captain Benjamin Hornigold in the Bahamas. The Bahamas was a hangout for pirates. They were safe on these islands and were treated well by the natives. The weather was sunny and warm. There were lots of merchant ships that sailed these waters. These, of course, were very tempting for pirates.

Hornigold and Teach liked each other as soon as they met. The young pirate joined Captain Hornigold's crew. The captain taught him how to be a great pirate. They sailed to America. The pirates found lots of treasure around Delaware and Virginia. They captured a French slave ship, *Concorde*, off the island of St. Vincent on November 28, 1717. Teach asked if he could have the ship. Hornigold gave it to him, maybe because he felt that the young man was ready to command his own ship. Or maybe he just knew that the young pirate would take the ship anyway!

Teach renamed the 200-ton ship *Queen Anne's Revenge*. He put forty cannons on his new vessel and then was ready for battle! He set sail for the Caribbean. The young pirate never forgot what he had been taught. He grew a long, thick black beard. He braided it and tied it off with black ribbons. This is how he came to be known as "Blackbeard." The big beard, combined with his wild black head of hair and dark mustache, made the pirate look scary.

Blackbeard attacked ships around the world. He became known as the "Black-faced Devil" and the "Fury from Hell." Before battle he stuck slow-burning fuses under his hat. When the fuses were lit, they made him look even scarier. Blackbeard never hurt people on the ships he attacked if they surrendered. But if they chose to fight, they were in trouble!

He knew a crew could become mutinous. A first mate could take command if the rest of the crew agreed. Blackbeard made sure this never happened to him. One night when his first mate and another crew member were in Blackbeard's cabin, Blackbeard pulled out a pistol. He shot his first mate, Israel Hands, in the kneecap. The man screamed in pain. He cried out "Why?" Blackbeard laughed before saying, "If I don't kill somebody now and then, you'll forget who I am!"

Israel Hands was a cripple because of the injury. Blackbeard kept the man on his crew. His crew would not dare turn mutinous after that!

The sea robber had one weakness. He loved women. He had fourteen wives! These were not real marriages. The pirate captain would bring his bride aboard the ship. One of his men conducted a sort of marriage ceremony. This meant they were not legally married. There was no shortage of women who wanted to be with the famous Blackbeard.

Blackbeard met pirate Captain Stede Bonnet in the Caribbean. The two became partners. Bonnet was not a good captain. His men were ready to mutiny. Teaming up with Blackbeard kept his crew happy.

Blackbeard wanted Bonnet's ship for his flotilla. His fleet of ships then included the forty-cannon *Queen Anne's Revenge*; Bonnet's ten-cannon sloop *Revenge*; and an eight-cannon sloop, *Adventure*. He also had a couple of smaller ships. He commanded more than three hundred men. Some sources say he commanded as many as 400 men!

By 1718, Blackbeard had looted lots of ships around St. Vincent, St. Lucia, Antigua, Puerto Rico, Hispaniola (Dominican Republic), Turneffe Islands (Bay of Honduras), Cuba, the Bahamas, and America.

That year the captain of one of Blackbeard's ships tried to capture the *Protestant Caesar,* a merchant ship that was commanded by Captain Wyar. Blackbeard's ten-cannon sloop *Revenge* was under Lt. Richard's command. Bonnet was the captain in name only. Richard attacked the *Protestant Caesar,*

Queen Anne's Revenge

Christened the *Concorde* when it was built in 1713, *Queen Anne's Revenge* was a French slave ship before Blackbeard and Hornigold captured it in 1717. Blackbeard renamed it *Queen Anne's Revenge,* probably because earlier he had fought in Queen Anne's War. It served as Blackbeard's main ship until it ran aground in June 1718. The ship is 80 to 100 feet long and 24.5 feet wide. It could carry 200 to 300 tons. The *Queen Anne's Revenge* held as many as forty cannons and up to 150 pirates. Blackbeard commanded this ship for only seven months. During that time, he captured at least eighteen ships.

For more than 280 years, the *Queen Anne's Revenge* has been on the ocean bottom awaiting discovery. For the past several years a company called Intersal has been working with the state of North Carolina to recover artifacts from a ship believed to be the *Queen Anne's Revenge*. The excavations began in November 1996, when a shipwreck was found near Beaufort Inlet (formerly Topsail Inlet). It will take several more years to get all the artifacts out of the water and study the shipwreck. That will give us a better idea of whether it is really Blackbeard's ship. A website has been set up to follow this excavation. Go to www.ncmaritime.org and then click on the picture of Blackbeard.

but Captain Wyar and his crew defeated the pirates. When Blackbeard heard this, he was mad. He decided to go after the merchant ship. When the crew aboard *Protestant Caesar* saw Blackbeard coming, they fled in smaller boats. Blackbeard took whatever he wanted from the ship. Then he burned it.

In May 1718, Blackbeard sailed to South Carolina. He threatened to attack Charleston if he did not get what he wanted! It became known as "Blackbeard's Blockade of Charleston." It started when he learned that some ships were ready to leave port. The pirate stayed at the entrance of the harbor to keep these ships from leaving. They could not get past his ships. This is called a blockade. He captured eight merchant ships during the blockade.

One was a really big prize, the *Crowley*. It had many important people on board. A member of the governor's council, Mr. Samuel Wragg, was a passenger on that ship. Blackbeard sent Wragg and two of his men to see South Carolina Governor Johnson. They gave him a letter from Blackbeard. In the letter he asked for a chest of medicine. Blackbeard warned that if he did not get the medicine by the deadline, he would kill everyone on the *Crowley*. He also said that he would fire upon Charleston (which was called Charles Town at that time).

The deadline passed. There was no answer. His men had not returned. Blackbeard got really angry. He decided to attack! He opened his gun ports and shouted orders to his men. Before he could attack, a boat was seen coming their way. When it got closer, Blackbeard saw that it was Samuel Wragg and the two pirates. His men yelled out that they had the medicine.

Blackbeard must have needed the medicine badly. Why else would he do such a crazy thing? Many of his men were probably very sick with or dying of diseases and battle wounds. Blackbeard let his *Crowley* prisoners go free. He did steal the cargo from each ship he captured during the blockade. The treasure included £1500 in gold and silver coins. Compared to today's dollars, that was about $300,000.* (Note that £ stands for British pounds, the money used in America then.)

Blackbeard went to North Carolina in June 1718 to get a pardon. He went to the governor of North Carolina because they were on friendly terms. He thought Governor Eden would help him since he knew the South Carolina governor would not. Everyone knew what he had done in Charleston. He had to get a pardon or he was in big trouble. He was sure Governor Eden would give him one. Some scholars think the governor was a partner of Blackbeard's. Pirates sold their stolen goods at a cheap price to merchants, and they also spent lots of money having a good time while in port. They were good for the economy! Blackbeard may have shared his plunder with Governor Eden.

Governor Eden might have liked Blackbeard. But South Carolina Governor Johnson and Virginia Governor Spotswood did not. They were fed up with pirates. They asked the British Royal Navy to stop these sea robbers. (Remember, this was before 1776, and the British were still in charge.)

Blackbeard had bigger problems. He had too many men. The large crew was good when he was attacking merchant ships on the open sea. But now there was less loot and it was being split too many ways. He had to get rid of some of

---

* There are many different ways to measure worth. Remember that this is not exact.

the men. The pirate captain sailed his flotilla into Topsail Inlet, North Carolina. He ran *Queen Anne's Revenge* and *Adventure* aground. Experts do not agree on whether Blackbeard did this by accident or on purpose.

Blackbeard sent Bonnet and some other men ashore. He told him to check on their pardons. After they left, Blackbeard robbed the *Revenge*. His men loaded the stuff onto the *Adventure*. This was not the same *Adventure* he grounded. He had two sloops named *Adventure*. He marooned eighteen of Bonnet's men on a sandbar. Then he headed to Bath, North Carolina. When Blackbeard got to Bath in June 1718, he learned his pardon had been granted.

The North Carolina governor performed a wedding ceremony for Blackbeard. He married a beautiful young woman named Mary Ormond. Blackbeard swore that he would give up piracy. He settled down in Bath, where he was a local celebrity. Blackbeard was happy with this life. But he missed being a pirate.

He set up a small smuggling operation on Ocracoke Island. But it was not enough excitement for him. By fall of that same year, he had gone back to being a pirate. Soon after he went back to his old ways, Blackbeard learned that the governor of Pennsylvania had issued an arrest warrant for him. Blackbeard left America and sailed to Bermuda.

On his way, Blackbeard captured two French merchant ships. They were full of sugar and cocoa. Selling the sugar and cocoa would bring him a lot of money. Blackbeard put the loot onto his ship. He put all the French crew onto one of the French merchant ships and sent them home. Then he sailed back to North Carolina along with the second French ship.

When he got to Ocracoke Island, he told Governor Eden and customs collector Tobias Knight that he had found the ship deserted but full of cargo! Eden and Knight split the money from the sale of the cocoa and sugar. The pirate set fire to the merchant ship. There would be no proof of piracy without the ship.

Virginia Governor Spotswood learned what Blackbeard had done. The governor said Blackbeard's pardon was no longer good because he had committed piracy. Blackbeard had committed piracy, but there was no proof of it. The crew members from the merchant ship he had robbed were back in France. The ship was destroyed. The stolen goods had been sold.

That did not stop Governor Spotswood. He asked the British Royal Navy to capture Blackbeard. He said the pirate had to be stopped. He did not tell the navy that he had no proof of piracy. The Royal Navy sent Captain Gordon and Lieutenant Maynard to Governor Spotswood. The governor found two good ships, *Jane* and *Ranger,* for them to use. Then all he had to do was find the pirate's hideout.

Blackbeard's quartermaster was arrested. Governor Spotswood made him tell them where Blackbeard was hiding. The quartermaster told the governor where Teach's Hole could be found. A reward of one hundred pounds was offered for Blackbeard's capture—dead or alive. Lt. Maynard wanted that reward. He set out in the two ships with fifty-eight men.

The two sloops were loaded with axes, muskets, pistols, and cutlasses. There were no cannons. Cannons were too heavy. The ships had to be light enough to go into the shallow waters where Blackbeard was hiding. Maynard and his men got to Teach's Hole at night. They had to wait until dawn to attack. What a long night that must have been!

At sunrise on November 22, 1718, the navy ships entered the inlet. It's believed that Blackbeard knew they were coming because the customs collector, Tobias Knight, had sent the pirate a warning note. Why didn't he leave?

Even if he did not get the warning note, the pirate would have seen the navy ships anchored near the inlet. They were there all night. So why didn't Blackbeard try to escape? He could have easily gotten away. No one knew these waters like he did. He knew he did not have enough men to fight. He only had part of his crew with him. He was outnumbered three to one. But Blackbeard never backed down from a fight.

When Maynard got close, the pirate set sail for Ocracoke Island. The battle was on! They yelled threats at each other. Lt. Maynard chased the pirate. He did not know this was all part of Blackbeard's plan. There were sandbars all around Ocracoke. The pirate planned to get Maynard's ships stuck on one. His plan worked. Both of Maynard's ships ran aground. Blackbeard then attacked the *Jane*. His men loaded their guns and cannons with iron bars and spikes. The bars and spikes splintered the ship's wooden mast. It ripped the sails to shreds, so the

Grenades were popular pirate weapons. They were made using a mixture of tar and rags. The mix was put into a small bottle and lit. The grenades used by Blackbeard were usually glass bottles filled with black powder and shrapnel. Boom!

sloop could not sail. Captain Gordon was killed. Most of the crew was injured or dead. Blackbeard planned to take care of the *Ranger* and Lt. Maynard next.

But the winds changed quickly. Blackbeard's ship also got stuck on a sandbar. He and his men tried to push their sloop off the sandbar. Maynard had been trying to free his ship too, of course. He had dumped everything he could into the water. The ship became light enough to get off the sandbar. The Royal Navy had lost one ship and lots of men. But Maynard still had thirty well-trained men against twenty-three pirates. The lieutenant was sure he could win.

As Maynard pulled up next to Blackbeard, the pirate threw hand grenades onto the navy ship. When the smoke cleared, no one was standing but Lt. Maynard. Blackbeard thought all the men had been injured or killed. The pirate captain jumped on board the navy ship. He was going to kill the man who dared to try to capture him.

Maynard had the pirate right where he wanted him—on his ship. Maynard knew it would be easier to win if he could do battle on his own ship instead of on the pirate ship.

As soon as Blackbeard's boots hit the deck, the military men came up from below deck. When Blackbeard's crew saw what was happening, they jumped aboard the navy sloop. The fighting did not last long.

Maynard and Blackbeard fired shots at each other. The pirate's shot missed. Maynard hit the pirate in the shoulder. The injured pirate grabbed his cutlass, and Maynard pulled out his sword. It broke at the first cross with Blackbeard's cutlass. Maynard threw it down. He pulled out a pistol and shot Blackbeard again. The pirate kept fighting! He swung his cutlass and nearly killed Lt. Maynard. Before he could complete the deadly swing, one of Maynard's men came up behind Blackbeard and sliced his throat.

Lieutenant Maynard got off another shot. The "Black-faced Devil" would not die. It took five gunshot wounds and twenty cutlass wounds to kill him. When the pirate crew saw their leader fall over, they surrendered. The short battle ended with ten dead pirates, nine wounded pirates, ten dead navy men, and twenty-four injured navy men.

A man in the hold of *Adventure* had laid a trail of gunpowder across the floor. Just as he was about to light the gunpowder, another man jumped him. They began fighting. The noise brought the navy men below deck. They found out that Blackbeard had told one of his trusted crew members, Caesar, to stay in the hold during the attack. Caesar was told to blow up the ship if the pirates lost. A prisoner had seen what was happening. He fought the pirate to stop him.

Maynard cut off Blackbeard's head and threw the body overboard. He hung the pirate's head from the bowsprit. It stayed there during the trip to Virginia. Maynard needed the pirate's head. It was proof he had killed Blackbeard so he could get the reward from Governor Spotswood.

Maynard found a letter aboard *Adventure* that was signed "T.K." This stood for Tobias Knight, who was the customs collector for North Carolina. The letter was to Blackbeard. It was proof that Knight had made a deal with the pirates to raid warehouses holding sugar, cocoa, indigo, cotton, and other booty. He shared the stolen goods with the pirates. The sale of the stolen goods was part of Maynard's reward. He did not get it for almost four years. It was held until the trial was over. Knight was found not guilty. He died soon after the trial.

The captured pirates were taken to Williamsburg, Virginia. They were tried on March 12, 1719. All but two were hanged.

Israel Hands received a king's pardon. It came just one day before his scheduled execution. He was the first mate that Blackbeard had shot in the leg. He lived the rest of his life as a beggar. Another crew member, Samuel Odel, was found not guilty. Odel convinced the court that he had been forced into piracy.

Blackbeard's two-year "reign of terror" in the Carolinas came to a bloody end.

Blackbeard Legends

Teach's Lights: Blackbeard said that no one, save the Devil and himself, knew where he had hidden his treasure. Whoever lived longer would get all the riches. On clear nights, the water around Blackbeard's old hideout, Teach's Hole at Ocracoke Island, has a strange shine. This is called "Teach's Lights." Legend has it that the lights can be seen when Blackbeard swims these waters looking for his head. Anyone who follows these lights will find Blackbeard's treasure. Beware! The Devil will be seated on top of the chest waiting to get his share.

Skull Cup of Blackbeard: When Lt. Maynard brought the pirate's head back to Virginia, it was hung from a pole at the harbor in

Hampton, Virginia. The skull was stolen from here. Some say friends of Blackbeard stole it. The skull supposedly turned up many years later in some secret society at Yale University, later ending up in North Carolina. At some point, the skull was apparently coated with silver and made into a cup.

Former North Carolina judge and author Charles H. Whedbee said he drank from this silver-plated skull in the 1930s. It was called "Blackbeard's Cup." The skull ended up with pirate enthusiast Edward Rowe Snow in 1949. After his death, his widow gave the skull to the Peabody Essex Museum in Salem, Massachusetts. It has also been on exhibit at the Mariners' Museum in Newport News, Virginia.

Legend of Blackbeard's Revenge: During one of his many visits to Bath, Blackbeard saw a beautiful girl. She had long, curly hair, blue eyes, and pretty skin. Blackbeard really liked this girl. He sent for her, but she sent him a polite rejection note:

> *While I am flattered at your attentions, sir, I am sure I cannot receive them for I belong to another. I am engaged to be married in a fortnight. Best Wishes, Mary.*

He had the girl brought to his room. He gave her a chance to change her mind. She told him no. The pirate let her leave. The girl thought that was the end of it.

Later that day, a lovely gold-and-wood box came for her. When she opened it, she screamed. There was nothing in the box but a human finger! A note was next to it. It said that was all she would ever see again of her fiancé. The note was signed by Blackbeard. The young man was never seen again.

The beautiful girl could not get over the death of her fiancé. Fishermen, sea captains, even a boatful of passengers on a dinner cruise say they have seen this woman down by the docks on the anniversary of the day the couple was to be married.

There is another ending to this tale. Some say the young lady was Mary Ormond and that she finally agreed to Blackbeard's proposal. He gave up piracy for a while. When he returned to it, the young bride hung out at the docks waiting for Blackbeard to come back.

For more about Blackbeard, check out: www.blackbeardlives.com

ANNE BONNY

Anne was born in Ireland. Her father moved the family to America soon after she was born. They lived in Charleston, South Carolina. Anne's father was a hard worker, so he was not home much. The child was raised by her mother. But she died when Anne was only thirteen.

Anne became a tomboy. Even though she didn't care how she dressed or looked, she was very pretty. Her skin was beautiful and she had long, curly red hair. Many boys wanted to court (go out with) her. Anne was not interested. She found most of the boys boring. Her father made her get engaged when she was nineteen. He thought it was time for her to get married.

Anne did not even like the young man. She ran away with a sailor named James Bonny and married him instead. She liked to go to the docks and watch the ships come and go. That's where she met the sailor.

They went to New Providence, in the Bahamas, and Anne soon realized that she did not love her husband. She met pirate Captain Jack Rackham, who was also known as Calico Jack. He had come to New Providence to get a king's pardon for piracy. It was love at first sight for Anne and Jack. They knew the only way to be together was to steal a ship and run away. That's what they did.

Anne pretended to be a man. Women weren't allowed to be pirates. They weren't even allowed to be on the ships. It wasn't hard to fool the crew. Anne wore loose clothing and a large hat. She tucked her hair under the hat and wore no makeup.

Before Anne became a pirate, she helped her father run his Charleston plantation. She was in charge of the kitchen. There was a servant girl that Anne didn't like. The servant didn't like Anne and would not do what Anne asked. This made Anne mad, and one day she supposedly got so angry that she killed the girl! If this story is true, it seems like Anne had the right personality to become a pirate.

The pirates attacked a few merchant ships. Some of the crew members from these merchant ships were forced to join the pirates. One of the new pirates began spending a lot of time with Anne. Captain Rackham became jealous. Anne had to tell him the truth. Her new friend was a woman who was also pretending to be a man! Anne's friend was Mary Read. The women decided not to hide their identities any longer. They let the other pirates know they were women. No one cared! The men knew these women were good pirates. One of the men fell in love with Mary. They got married.

Their ship was attacked at Point Negril, Jamaica. They were at the dock when it happened. British Captain Barnet had been sent by the Jamaican government. He was told to capture any pirates he found. The pirates were no match for the military. Mary and Anne were the only ones willing to fight. The women yelled for the men to come up and help. The men were below deck too drunk and sleepy to fight. They didn't help the women. All of the pirates were captured and taken to Port Royal, Jamaica.

Captain Rackham was found guilty of piracy and was eventually hanged. Mary Read's husband said that he had been forced into piracy and was found not guilty of piracy. Mary and Anne were both found guilty. They would have been hanged, but both said they were pregnant. They were sentenced to life in prison.

Anne Bonny was sent back to Charleston in 1721. Some believe that her father paid Bahamas Governor Rogers a lot of money to let her out of prison. Historians do not know what happened to Anne. She never returned to piracy, however. She must have missed those exciting days at sea.

JOHN "CALICO JACK" RACKHAM

John Rackham was the first mate of English pirate Captain Charles Vane. He told the rest of the crew that he would be a better leader. The other pirates believed him. They decided to mutiny and told Vane that he was no longer the captain. The mutineers put Vane and some of his loyal men into a small boat. John Rackham was the new captain!

War broke out between England and Spain during the early eighteenth century. Captain Rackham wanted to be a privateer in this war. He had to get a pardon for piracy before the king would let him be a privateer. He went to New Providence, an island in the Bahamas that was very popular with pirates, to get the pardon. He met Anne Bonny while waiting for his pardon.

It was love at first sight. Suddenly Rackham didn't care about the pardon anymore. He and Anne decided to run away so they could be together. Rackham rounded up eight men. He found a ship that had enough guns and was fast enough for piracy. When the time was right, he stole the ship.

He renamed the stolen ship *Curlew*. Anne became part of the crew. She dressed like a man. It was the only way she could be on the ship. Women were not allowed to be pirates. They sailed around the West Indies. The pirates attacked any ships they could find. One of the first ships they captured was a Dutch merchant ship. They forced the crew to join them as pirates. Anne Bonny became friends with one of the new pirates. Captain Rackham did not like this and became jealous. Anne had to tell him that her new friend was also a woman!

Over the next few months the pirates were nearly caught several times. They thought they would be safer in North Carolina. They found out that was not really true. While North Carolina still welcomed pirates, nearby South Carolina and Virginia did not. Officials in those two colonies had already captured and hanged many pirates.

Captain Rackham took his crew to Jamaica. They attacked a merchant ship. The same ship had been robbed by pirates less than a month before. This was too much. The governor of Jamaica sent the Royal Navy after the pirates. The navy men found the ship in the port. The crew members

Women were not usually allowed on pirate ships. That is why Anne Bonny and Mary Read had to pretend they were men until they proved themselves in battle.

were all on board. When the pirates realized what was happening, only two pirates really fought. Mary Read and Anne Bonny tried to get the other pirates to help, but most of the men did not.

Captain Rackham and another crew member fought for a few minutes, but they knew they were no match for the Royal Navy. They hid below deck. The women were so mad that they fired shots into the hold! The men yelled at the women to stop. Anne and Mary shouted insults at the men.

Finally the women had to surrender. The pirates were taken to St. Jago de la Vega, Jamaica, for trial. Calico Jack Rackham was found guilty of piracy. On November 17, 1720, he was hanged at Gallows Point in Port Royal, Jamaica. Anne and Calico Jack saw each other before his execution. Anne was still mad at Captain Rackham when she visited him. She told him, ". . . if you had stayed and fought like a man, you need not be hanged like a dog."

MARY READ

Like Anne Bonny, Mary Read was a tomboy when she was a teenager. A tomboy acts more like a boy than a girl. She dressed and acted like a boy to get a job. Girls did not work back then, but Mary wanted to make money to help her mother pay the bills. Mary got her first job when she was fourteen years old. She did chores and ran errands for an elderly woman. When she was old enough, Mary joined the military. She had to dress and act like a young man or she would not have been accepted. Her disguise worked! She became a cadet in the British Army.

Mary learned many skills. She learned how to use a knife as a weapon and how to shoot a gun. She was tough and brave. Mary fell in love with another soldier, but he did not know Mary was a woman. After she told him that she was a woman, he fell in love with her.

Their captain got honorable discharges for them. They were able to leave the military early without being punished. The couple got married. Mary Read wore a dress for the first time at her wedding. She and her husband opened a tavern in Brabant, Holland. The couple had a good life. The two were happy until Mary's husband became ill and died.

Soon after his death, business got bad. The tavern began losing money. In her early twenties, Mary decided to become a merchant marine. She joined a Dutch merchant ship that was on its way to the West Indies. The ship was captured by pirates. They made the crew become pirates too. Mary had lots of adventures while she was a pirate.

By 1718, Mary Read had accepted the king's pardon. Pardons were granted when the government forgave people for being pirates. But they

A doctor never saw a new military recruit in the 1700s. Right after a young man joined the military, he was given an assignment. There was no doctor's exam to make sure he was fit for duty! Sailors also did not bathe much or dress in front of others. All of these things made it easy for a woman wearing loose clothing, a big hat, and no makeup to pass for a young man.

could no longer be pirates. Mary ran out of money a few months later. She heard that the governor of the Bahamas, Woodes Rogers, was looking for privateers. She joined his crew. She had to dress and act like a man once more. The ship was taken over by pirate Captain "Calico Jack" Rackham. Mary became a pirate again.

Mary did not know that there was another female pirate on this ship, but Anne Bonny was also pretending to be a man. The women became best friends. They learned each other's secret.

Captain Rackham did not like his girlfriend spending so much time with what he thought was another man. He got angry. Anne had to tell Rackham that her friend was a woman.

The pirates attacked another merchant ship, and its crew was also forced into piracy. One of the men was an Englishman named Tom Deane. Deane and Read became good friends. She told him that she was a woman. They fell in love. Anne Bonny and Mary Read eventually told the whole crew they were women. The pirates didn't care. By then they knew Anne and Mary were good pirates.

The pirates attacked ships in the Indies and in America. Then they went back to Jamaica. They hung out at the island of Hispaniola.

In November 1720, the pirates were attacked by the military. The pirates were not ready to fight. Most were asleep after a long night of partying. They either could not be awakened or were unwilling to fight. Mary Read and Anne Bonny fought but lost.

The pirates were taken prisoner. There was a trial. Mary Read and Anne Bonny were found guilty of piracy. Both women told the judge they were pregnant, so they were not hanged. They were given life in prison instead. Mary Read became ill with fever. She died in a Jamaican jail in 1721. Her husband, Tom Deane, was found not guilty. He told the judge he had been forced into piracy.

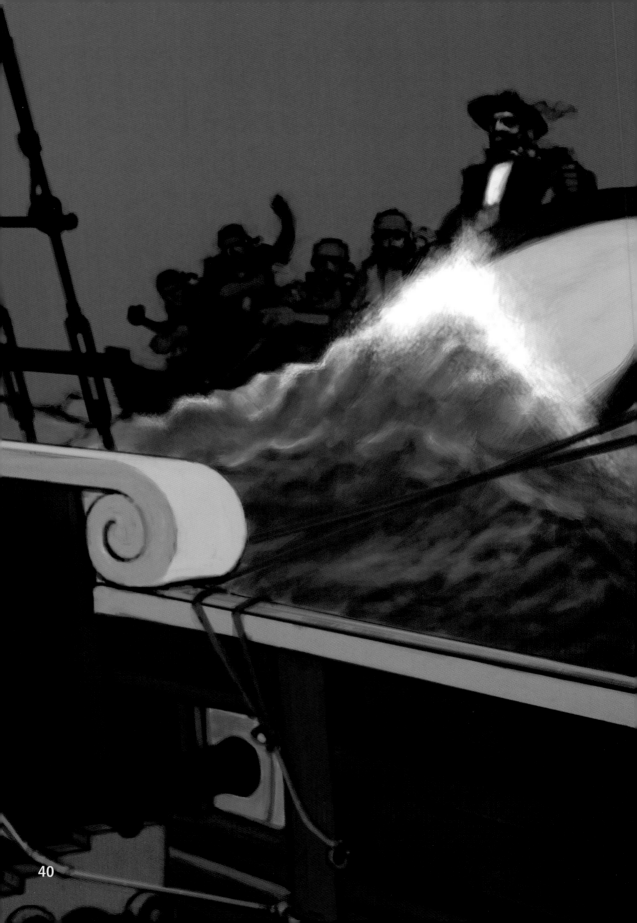

HENRY "LONG BEN" AVERY (ALSO KNOWN AS THE "ARCH PIRATE")

Henry Avery was born in England in 1653. He hated school but loved the sea. The boy ran away and joined the crew of a ship going to America. He got into trouble during the trip. The captain locked him in the hold until they got to Carolina. Records do not say whether it was North or South Carolina. The boy was ordered off the ship in Carolina.

He went back to England three years later on a merchant ship. His father had died while he was gone. His mother died soon after he came home. Avery was placed under the care of a local merchant, Mr. Lightfoot. The man could no longer take care of the boy when his business failed, so Avery lived on the streets. He stole to survive. The young man soon returned to life at sea.

Avery became first mate on a privateering ship called the *Duke*. He started a mutiny against Captain Gibson. The captain and some of his men were put into a lifeboat. Avery became a captain at only twenty years old.

Captain Avery renamed the ship *Fancy*. He sailed to Madagascar. On the way, he wrote a letter and sent it when he got to this pirate port. It said that all English captains should beware. He had a ship with 46 guns and a crew of 150 men. He warned that if they did not stay out of his way, he would fight them to the death. The letter was a warning. Merchant ships that did not surrender would be in big trouble.

Two other pirates, Captain Tew and Captain Mission, joined Avery. The pirates attacked ships around Madagascar, the West Indies, Newfoundland, and the Arabian Coast. They were very successful. Avery took on other names, including "Long Ben."

In September 1695, the pirates attacked the biggest ship of the Great Mogul's fleet, *Gang-i-Sawai*. They captured it in the Gulf of Aden at the mouth of the Red Sea. The ship had six hundred people on board. Many were important people from the emperor's court. The ship was loaded down with cargo.

The emperor of India was called the Great Mogul between the fifteenth and eighteenth centuries. The Great Mogul had many valuable things on the ship Avery attacked: big gold plates, fine fabrics, bags of gold and silver coins, a jewel-studded saddle that was handmade for the Mogul, and lots of diamonds.

Avery told the other pirate captains that the loot should stay on his ship, *Fancy*. He said the *Fancy* was the fastest sloop. If there were trouble, he would be able to escape. While the other pirates were asleep, Captain Henry "Long Ben" Avery and his men set sail. They took all of the plunder with them. It was worth £325,000, which would be about $58.6 million today. Each member of Avery's crew received £2,000. That would be the same as about $360,500 today.

The Great Mogul was angry when he learned about the pirate attack. He stopped all trade with England. The Mogul wanted Avery punished. When the pirate arrived in the Bahamas, he learned what was happening. Avery tried to bribe Bahamas Governor Trott. The governor told Avery that he could not pardon him. He warned him there was a big reward for his capture.

The pirates split up. Some went to America. Some went to England and Ireland. Twenty-four pirates were caught. Six were hanged. So what happened to Henry Avery?

Avery ended up back in England. He had taken his share of the loot in diamonds. He had to sell them to diamond merchants. He asked some old friends to take his diamonds to the merchants. He could not go himself because he was a wanted man. His friends took the bag of diamonds to Bristol.

Avery stayed in Biddiford. It was a small town where he could safely hide. He waited for his friends. They never came back. Avery knew something was wrong. He had no choice but to go to Bristol. When he got there he learned his friends had sold the diamonds. But then they had run away with the money! Henry Avery died a few years later, a poor man.

WILLIAM "BILLY" LEWIS

By the time he was eleven, Billy Lewis was a pirate! He met a pirate named Captain Banister while he was hanging out at Boston Harbor. Lewis joined his crew. The youth loved being part of a pirate crew. When the ship was captured by the British Royal Navy, though, Billy Lewis said that he had been forced into piracy. His best friend, Darby McCaffrey, said the same thing. The rest of the pirates were tried in Port Royal, Jamaica, on charges of piracy. Lewis and McCaffrey were freed.

The teenagers soon joined a merchant ship. The pair sailed around the world for five years. The ship was captured by Spanish pirates at Havana, Cuba.

The pirates worked Lewis and McCaffrey like slaves. Living conditions on the ship were bad. It was hard to get enough food to eat. The boys did not want to live this way anymore. They, along with six other pirates, escaped in a canoe. The group captured a Spanish boat. Some of the men from that crew joined the pirates.

Billy Lewis was now captain of forty men. Darby McCaffrey was his quartermaster. Captain Lewis soon found a ten-gun sloop on its way to the Bay of Campeachy. He sent a note to its captain that said, "Sell your ship for 10,000 pieces of eight or face the consequences."

When Captain Tucker read the note, he knew he was in big trouble. He talked to other captains. He tried to get them to help him stop the pirates. Tucker warned them that his ship was just the first to be targeted by the pirates. Soon they would come after other ships too.

The other captains did not want to fight the pirates for some reason. But they did not leave the area, either. Maybe they did not think the pirates would really attack them. Captain Tucker got away. The other ten ships that would not help him were captured! One ship surrendered as soon as Billy Lewis's pirates fired a shot. Many of its crew members became pirates. Lewis doubled the number of men in his crew. He went from forty men to eighty men.

Captain Lewis picked the best ship of his new flotilla to be his flagship. It was a 90-ton sloop that held twelve cannons. He gave it a new name, *Morning Star*. He and his crew took prizes all along the southeastern seaboard. They found lots of loot in Florida and South Carolina.

We do not know if Lewis was French or English. He spoke French, Spanish, English, and some Indian dialects.

Captain Lewis left South Carolina. He robbed ships in the waters around Virginia for a while before going back to South Carolina. Then he sailed to Newfoundland and Conception Bay. He captured a ship called the *Herman* that had twenty-four guns. Captain Beal of this ship promised to give Lewis supplies if he would not attack them. He told Captain Lewis to send his quartermaster to him to get the supplies. The pirate sent Darby McCaffrey to get the supplies from the *Herman*'s captain.

But it was a trick! Darby was captured and taken to the governor of the Bahamas, Woodes Rogers. When Captain Lewis found out what had happened, he attacked a couple of ships. He took all aboard as his prisoners. Captain Beal's brother was one of the prisoners. The pirate captain sent word to Captain Beal and Governor Rogers that he would kill the man if Captain Beal did not let Darby McCaffrey go. The quartermaster was freed! Lewis let his prisoners go too.

Not long after, Captain Lewis attacked a French ship. This was a big win. Lewis was now the leader of more than two hundred men. He had several ships (and dozens of cannons) in his flotilla. But the prize came at a great cost. His best friend and quartermaster, Darby McCaffrey, was killed during the attack.

Lewis did not take the death of his friend well. He began to act recklessly. He headed for Guinea. He attacked all ships he came across. Lewis did not talk to his men anymore. He kept to himself most of the time. The pirate began talking to himself. The crew members did not like the change in their leader. They thought Lewis was talking to the Devil.

In the waters around South Carolina, the ship lost part of its masts. Captain Lewis and his crew were after a merchant ship. The loss of the sails slowed the pirate ship down. They were not going to catch the ship they were after. Lewis climbed up the sails to the torn topmast. When he got to the top, he pulled out some of his hair. He held it up to the sky. "Good Devil, take this until I come!" he screamed at the top of his lungs.

After that, the ship picked up speed. The pirates soon overtook the other ship. They won the battle. His men believed Lewis had made a deal with the Devil. Some of his loyal men tried to warn their captain. Lewis would not listen, though. He answered them by saying, "When the Devil comes to claim my soul, there is nothing anyone can do to prevent it."

Some of the crew members came into his cabin that night. They murdered Captain William Lewis while he was asleep.

Code of Conduct

Every captain had rules for his men. These rules were called their Code of Conduct. These were pirate Captain Bartholomew Roberts' rules. (He was known as "Black Bart.")

1. Every man gets a vote. Every man gets the same food and drink. Food and drink will be rationed if supplies get low.
2. Every man gets a share of a prize. A man will be marooned if caught stealing.
3. No betting money on card or dice games.
4. Lights out at 8 P.M.
5. Pistols and cutlasses must be clean and ready for battle.
6. No boy or woman is allowed on the ship.
7. All pirates must fight during battle. If a pirate hides or leaves the ship during battle, he will be marooned or killed.
8. No fighting each other on the ship.
9. If a man loses an arm or leg, he will get 800 pieces of eight.
10. The captain and quartermaster each get two shares of a prize. The sailing master, boatswain, and gunner each get one and a half shares. The other officers each get one and a quarter. All other crew members get one share each.
11. Musicians have Sundays off. They must play the other six days and nights.

STEDE "THE GENTLEMAN PIRATE" BONNET

Stede Bonnet was an officer in the colonial militia. After his service, he lived at his family's plantation in Barbados. Bonnet grew sugarcane. He was good at it but did not enjoy it. He was bored with his new life. He missed the action of the militia. One day Bonnet surprised everyone. He bought a ship and became a pirate!

Bonnet named his ship *Revenge.* He equipped it with ten guns. He chose as his quartermaster an old sea dog, Israel Morton. Morton rounded up seventy pirates for their crew.

Captain Bonnet got off to a great start as a pirate. He attacked three ships and got many good prizes. Bonnet set fire to every ship he captured. This kept his pirating activities and location a secret. After all, without a ship, there was no evidence a pirate had done anything wrong. No ship also meant that it was harder to track down a pirate. Things went well for Bonnet until he got to the Carolinas. Bonnet could not find any plunder there.

His crew was fed up with him. The men did not think he was a good leader. They did not like the fancy clothes their captain wore. They called him the "Gentleman Pirate" behind his back. Bonnet did not drink. The men in his crew loved to drink. But the worst thing was that Captain Bonnet got seasick. He tried to hide it, but his men knew. They had no respect for a captain who got sick at sea! He was losing control of his men.

Before the men turned mutinous, Bonnet ran into Blackbeard. The famous pirate found Bonnet amusing. What Blackbeard really liked was Bonnet's sloop. Blackbeard added the *Revenge* to his flotilla. At first, Bonnet believed that he and Blackbeard were partners. He found out he was wrong when Blackbeard put one of his own men in command of the *Revenge.* Bonnet did not really mind. He knew he and his men were not likely to be attacked as long as Blackbeard was their leader.

Soon after they joined forces, Blackbeard attacked Charleston. This was his famous Blockade of Charleston. Not long after this happened, Blackbeard knew he had to get rid of some of his crew. He had too many

Stede Bonnet liked to wear fancy clothes. He wore nice pants and a white shirt with a ruffled front and oversized sleeves. And he always wore colorful vests.

ships and men. He was not getting as much loot in the Carolinas as he was at sea. He had to divide what loot they did get between many men.

Blackbeard told Bonnet he needed to careen his flagship, *Queen Anne's Revenge*. This meant pulling the ship ashore to do a lot of cleaning and repairs. Blackbeard said they should hide until they got the pardons they had asked for after the Charleston attack. Blackbeard took all his ships into Beaufort Inlet. It was called Topsail Inlet at that time. He sent Bonnet and his men ashore to check on the pardons. Bonnet did not want to leave his ship. But he knew better than to cross Blackbeard. He left some of his men behind to watch Blackbeard.

Blackbeard had his men move everything valuable off Bonnet's ship onto one of his smaller ships. Then Blackbeard set sail for England. He stopped long enough to maroon Bonnet's ship on a sandbar with his men aboard.

When Bonnet came back, he saw what Blackbeard had done. He rescued his ship and men. Then he went in search of Blackbeard. It was a good thing he did not find him because Bonnet was no match for Blackbeard!

Bonnet changed his name to Captain Thomas. He did this because his pardon was in the name of Stede Bonnet and he didn't want to lose the pardon. He renamed his ship *Royal James*. He captured many great prizes around Delaware Bay and Virginia. Eventually it came time to careen his ship. He chose a cove near the mouth of the Cape Fear River.

South Carolina Governor Johnson learned where the pirate was hiding. The governor sent Colonel William Rhett to capture him. Colonel Rhett led two eight-gun sloops, *Henry* and *Sea Nymph*. He had a crew of 130 men.

Bonnet's ship got stuck on a sandbar as he tried to flee. Rhett's ship also got stuck on the sandbar. They fought for hours before Bonnet surrendered. The pirates were brought to Charleston.

Bonnet and his sailing master, David Herriot, escaped from prison. They had not been well guarded. The authorities did not think that the Gentleman Pirate would try to escape. They thought he would want to answer the charges against him. It did not help him when the authorities learned that he had already gotten a pardon. They did not like that he had been pardoned but remained a pirate. Governor Johnson offered a £700 reward (about $135,000 in today's money) for the capture of Stede Bonnet and Herriot—dead or alive.

Bonnet and Herriot stole a boat to escape. Colonel Rhett found them before they got far. Herriot was killed during the attack. Bonnet was once again arrested. He was taken to Charleston. The judge found him guilty. Justice Trott made a long speech about how Bonnet was no gentleman. Trott said that he deserved to be hanged.

On November 8, 1718, Stede "the Gentleman Pirate" Bonnet and all of his men but three were hanged at White Point in Charleston.

CHARLES VANE

A Spanish galleon filled with treasure ran into a reef and sank near Florida in about 1716. Many pirates tried to find the treasure. Another Spanish galleon was sent to get the treasure. Two Spanish warships were also sent to protect the galleon and keep pirates from attacking.

The treasure was loaded onto the Spanish galleon. The warships left. That is when pirate Captain Charles Vane attacked the ship and got the treasure.

Woodes Rogers, the governor of New Providence (Bahamas), had a goal to end piracy. Rogers gave pardons to pirates in hopes that they would quit piracy. The governor said that sea robbers were no longer welcome. This had been a favorite pirate hangout. Charles Vane had thought he was safe, but now he was trapped there with a big treasure. Not knowing what else to do, Vane wrote a letter to the governor. He agreed to accept the pardon if he could keep his treasure.

The letter made Governor Woodes Rogers really mad. There was no way he would give a pardon and let a pirate keep what he had stolen. Rogers blocked the pirate's ship as he was trying to escape. The smart pirate set fire to another ship. The governor's men were so busy trying to move their ship away from the one on fire that the pirates sailed away with the treasure!

Vane had escaped in a sloop owned by a man named Yeates. On his way to America, Captain Vane captured a ship from Barbados. He made Yeates commander of it. Vane headed for Hispaniola, and on the way he captured a Spanish ship off St. Christopher. Vane took the loot back to North Carolina, which was still friendly toward pirates.

Before becoming the governor of the Bahamas, Woodes Rogers was a privateer. A musket ball shattered his jaw during a battle. He was disfigured from the bad injury. Woodes Rogers was sent to the Bahamas to end piracy. This was quite a job since pirates loved to hang out in the Bahamas!

The pirates took whatever they wanted in those days. Merchant ships at the port of Charleston were in the most danger. Vane had a crew of over a hundred men. Yeates declared mutiny against Vane. He took his ship and crew and escaped into the Edisto River. Vane followed, but Yeates shot at his ship. Vane knew it would be better to catch Yeates by surprise. Vane found Blackbeard while looking for an inlet where he could wait. Vane and his men joined the big pirate party at Ocracoke Island.

Yeates and his men got pardons while Vane was at Ocracoke. Yeates snitched that Charles Vane was in the area. South Carolina Governor Johnson sent Colonel William Rhett and his men to capture him. The pirate captain was gone by the time they arrived. Near Delaware, Vane encountered a warship. His men wanted him to attack, but he did not. Vane knew they would not win. His first mate, John "Calico Jack" Rackham, thought they could have captured the warship.

Many of the men agreed with Rackham. A vote was taken. Should Charles Vane remain their captain or should his first mate take over as leader? The crew members elected Rackham as their new captain. Near Jamaica, the new captain put Vane and some of his loyal men into a schooner. He let them sail away.

It was not long before Vane made a comeback. He got some guns and took a few good prizes. At the Bay of Honduras, Vane's ships were thrown onto some rocks during a storm. Many of the men were killed instantly. The others drowned.

The only survivor was Charles Vane. He made it to a deserted island. Turtle hunters in small canoes gave Vane fresh water. The pirate caught fish and ate bananas to survive.

One day a merchant ship passed by Vane's island. The ship's leader, Captain Holford, was one of Vane's old shipmates. What good luck! Holford had been a pirate, but he got a pardon and gave it up. The merchant captain would not take the pirate aboard. What bad luck! Holford did not trust the pirate.

Holford said he would return in a month. He would take Vane as a prisoner to Port Royal, Jamaica. Another merchant captain stopped at the island. Vane said he was a shipwrecked sailor. He was taken aboard as a new crew member. The ship passed Captain Holford's ship. More bad luck!

This captain was friends with Captain Holford. He invited Holford on board. Holford saw Charles Vane. He told the captain who Vane really was. Holford took Vane as a prisoner and then turned him in to the authorities at Port Royal.

Charles Vane was tried on March 22, 1720. Vane pleaded not guilty. At the end of the trial, the verdict was read. Charles Vane was found guilty of piracy, felony, and robbery.

The pirate was hanged on March 29, along with two other pirates, at Gallows Point in Port Royal, Jamaica.

There were two types of pirate flags. One was a red flag (called a "Red Jack"). It was a warning to surrender so that no one would be harmed. The other type of flag was a black flag ("Jolly Roger"). The word "roger" means rogue or rover. The Jolly Roger flag meant that the victims would all die if they did not surrender. The pictures on the flags were personalized. This meant they were symbols of each pirate captain. The designs often had crossed bones, skulls, skeletons, and cutlasses.

WILLIAM KIDD
Pirate or Privateer?

William Kidd was born in Greenock, Scotland, in about 1645. He was the son of a poor minister. When he was old enough, he went to sea. He later joined a pirate ship called the *Blessed William*. The Royal Navy caught up with this ship in the Caribbean. After a short battle, the pirates had to surrender.

Kidd got a pardon from the king. Then he became a privateer in King William's War (1689-1697). He made lots of money as a privateer.

When the war was over, Kidd became a sea captain and then a merchant in New York City. He married a beautiful woman named Sarah. They had two daughters. William Kidd loved his family but longed for life at sea.

He met a businessman, Robert Livingston, who was also from Scotland. They became friends. Livingston asked Kidd if he would be interested in a business deal with the English king, William III. He said it was a get-rich scheme. Their partner would be Lord Bellomont, who was governor of Barbados then.

The more Kidd thought about it, the more he liked the plan. He missed his days as a privateer. This was a chance to be one again. It was also a chance to get rich. He said yes.

Lord Bellomont, Robert Livingston, and William Kidd thought the plan was worth the risk. Kidd thought they would get rich beyond their wildest dreams. Bellomont and his secret partners would get fifty percent of the plunder. Ten percent would go to the king of England. The rest would be divided among Captain Kidd, Livingston, and the crew.

The agreement was clear. If no plunder was found, Captain Kidd and Robert Livingston would have to pay back all the money their partners had given them. This would put Livingston and Kidd in debt. No plunder would also mean no pay for the crew. This was called, "No prey, no pay."

Kidd went to England in 1695 to get two commissions from the king. One commission allowed him to capture pirates. The other allowed him to attack French ships, since England and France were at war.

Kidd had a great, fast ship. The *Adventure Galley* weighed 287 tons and was 125 feet long, with three masts and many cannons. Its three huge sails were made using 3,200 yards of canvas. The ship had thirty-two oars

to row the ship in case there was no wind. Kidd needed 150 men. He could only find seventy good sailors. He had trouble finding more good men. He decided to get the rest of his crew in New York.

The privateer had trouble before he even left England. He passed a Royal Navy ship on its way to the English Channel. Kidd did not dip his colors (lower his flag) to show respect to the Royal Navy. Worse still, some members of his crew actually turned their backs to the navy ship and slapped their rear ends! This was very disrespectful. The Royal Navy stopped Kidd's ship. Naval authorities took many of his men as punishment.

Kidd was not worried. He was sure he could get all the men he needed in New York. He left England and sailed to America. However, it turned out that he was not able to find good men in New York either. Captain Kidd had to take thugs, vagabonds, and pirates. He even had to take gentlemen with no sailing experience. These men were attracted by the excitement of this mission. They also thought they would get rich.

Kidd set sail for Madagascar, Malabar, and the Red Sea area. He ran into the Royal Navy again in December 1696 near Capetown, Africa. By the time they got to Madagascar, the ship was leaking. Supplies were low. Kidd's men were unhappy. Things got worse. Fifty men got sick and died. Captain Kidd had to take thirty pirates aboard his ship as crew members in Madagascar just to have enough men to work the ship.

They sailed from Madagascar to the Red Sea. They found no pirates. They saw no French merchant ships. Kidd attacked what he thought was a French ship. When it turned out to be an English ship, *Sceptre,* under the command of English Captain Barlow, he let it go. Kidd's unhappy crew watched the merchant ship and all its plunder sail away. Then he had the bad luck to attack another English ship, *Loyal Captain*. When he apologized and let yet another ship filled with cargo sail away, his crew was nearly mutinous.

Most of Captain Kidd's men thought he should have kept the cargo from the English ship. A gunner named William Moore said this to Captain Kidd in front of the rest of the crew. This was very disrespectful. Kidd got angry. The two men began to yell at each another. Captain Kidd got so mad that he threw a big bucket at William Moore. It hit him hard in the head, and Moore died from the injury.

Kidd and his men went on to attack a few more ships, though they

Passes (flags) were sometimes used to fool other ships. Both privateers and merchants tried to trick each other by raising phony passes. Privateers would raise the pass of the ship they wanted to attack. Captain Kidd had the right to attack French ships. He raised a French flag when he saw a French ship.

Merchant ships did the same thing. They raised false passes to protect their cargo. If a privateer saw they were both English, the privateer might leave the merchant ship alone. This is why Captain Kidd attacked English ships twice. The English ships raised false passes so they would not be attacked. If they had shown their true English passes, Kidd would have left them alone.

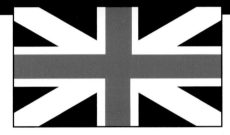

did not have much plunder aboard. These ships did not turn out to be French either, so Captain Kidd had no right to attack them. But his men were sick of letting ships go and not taking their plunder. Kidd feared his men would mutiny, so he let them attack the ships anyway.

At this point the British government was very angry with Kidd. It had been eighteen months since he left England, and Captain Kidd had nothing to show for it. He had no prizes from French ships and had not captured any pirates.

And then he saw a large merchant ship on the horizon that looked like it was loaded down with plunder. On January 30, 1698, Captain Kidd gave the orders and attacked it.

When he went aboard, he found out it was not a French ship. It was the *Quedagh Merchant* and belonged to the Great Mogul of India. Kidd robbed it anyway. Gold, silver, jewels, silks, and food were loaded onto Captain Kidd's ship.

The Great Mogul stopped all trade with England after Kidd's attack. The ruler demanded that England punish Captain Kidd for attacking the *Quedagh Merchant*. Kidd did not know any of this when he started the voyage home in June of 1698.

Kidd knew he had some explaining to do and that he needed to get home as fast as possible. The *Adventure Galley* was no longer seaworthy. He took the *Quedagh Merchant* for the long voyage instead. He renamed the stolen ship the *Adventure Prize*. He and a small crew headed for America. When the ship reached the Caribbean, he learned how much trouble he was in. They were calling him a pirate! Kidd was worried, but he was sure that his good friend Lord Bellomont would come to his aid.

Kidd got rid of the *Adventure Prize* in the Caribbean. He bought a fast sloop, *Antonio*. It had been more than three years since he had been in New York. Kidd sailed into New York's harbor in June 1699.

He learned that Bellomont had become governor of New York, New Hampshire, and Massachusetts Bay. Kidd sent a friend of his to talk to Bellomont. His friend was a lawyer, James Emmott. Emmott told Bellomont all about what had happened during Captain Kidd's voyage. The lawyer gave Bellomont the two commissions the king of England had given Kidd.

At first Bellomont said he would help Kidd. He asked Kidd to come see him and to bring his logbook. Captain Kidd said it had been destroyed by his crew. Governor Bellomont told Kidd to write a report of everything that had happened during his voyage. But when Kidd went to Bellomont's home to give him the report, he was arrested! He was kept in Boston's Stone Prison. Some of his loot was found and sent back to England. His partners, especially Bellomont, did not want anything to do with Captain Kidd, who was now considered a pirate.

On May 8, 1701, the trial of William Kidd began in London, England. He was not ready for it. He had not been allowed to have visitors. He was not given pen and paper to make notes. He was not given a lawyer until the

Edgar Allan Poe's story "The Gold Bug'" is about buried treasure on Sullivan's Island, South Carolina. In the story, a young boy is sent to Charleston to spend the summer with his uncle. The boy discovers Sullivan's Island and spends time there. He finds the island is not deserted after all. A man and his servant are there looking for Captain Kidd's buried treasure. They ask for the boy's help because he knows the island so well. They find the great treasure. The boy is sent back to the mainland. He has to get bags big enough to carry the treasure. When he comes back with the bags, the men are dead and the treasure is missing! It is said that Captain Kidd placed a curse on this treasure. No one who finds it will live to tell about it.

Captain Kidd's treasure was worth a lot of money. Many experts say it was as much as £710,000 (about $123 million in today's money). Some say it was much less. What we do know is that Kidd's treasure consisted of at least sixty pounds of gold; one hundred pounds of silver; and about $1.7 million's worth of fabric (in today's money), including muslins, brocades, and silks.

trial began. Kidd was also really sick from the terrible conditions in both the Boston prison and Newgate Prison in London.

The two commissions were missing. They were important evidence on Kidd's behalf. If they had been shown, his accusers would not have been able to charge him for piracy on two ships that had falsely flown French flags. He swore he gave the papers to Bellomont. Bellomont had died by the time the trial began. The papers were not found in Bellomont's belongings.

Kidd was also charged with the murder of William Moore, the gunner that he had hit with the bucket. Two of his crew testified against Kidd.

The trial lasted only two days. Captain William Kidd was found guilty of murder and five counts of piracy. His sentence was death. He was hanged on May 23, 1701, at a spot on the Thames River in London called Execution Dock. His hanging drew a huge crowd of spectators.

Was Kidd really a pirate or just a privateer who was a victim of his circumstances? He had a mutinous crew, partners who betrayed him for political reasons, an unfair trial, and an impossible mission. But he was not blameless. He was greedy for money and adventure and made many mistakes.

Captain Kidd hid some of his treasure on Gardiners Island in New York. Most or all of this treasure was found. It is believed that Kidd hid some of his treasure in the Carolinas too. It may be buried on North Carolina's Money Island or on Sullivan's Island (near Charleston), South Carolina.

John Redfield was an old friend of Captain Kidd's. He was with him on his final voyage. Captain Kidd asked Redfield to do him a favor. He asked his friend to guard his treasure. Kidd gave him these instructions:

I leave with you two chests. If I have not contacted you within the next five years, you may dig up one of the chests and help yourself to half its contents. If at the end of ten years' time you have not heard from me, you may dig up the second chest and take half of its contents. I want you to remain in this area. Here is one thousand pounds for your participation.

They buried the two treasure chests on a small island. Redfield found a wife in Charleston. He built a nice house. During the spring of 1701, a ship flying Captain Kidd's flag came to their island. The ship's captain was Max Brisbau, who had been one of Captain Kidd's crew members. Redfield invited the pirate into his home. Brisbau said that he had been sent by Kidd to get his treasure.

Redfield knew the man was lying. There was a secret signal that would have been given if he had really been sent by Captain Kidd. The pirate got very mad because Redfield would not tell him about the treasure. Captain Brisbau took Redfield and his wife aboard his ship. After the ship had been sailing for a long time, Captain Brisbau said, "Tell me where the treasure is or prepare to be thrown overboard! Now!"

The authorities pulled along the ship. They saw that the man and his wife were prisoners. They arrested the pirates and took their ship. Soon after this happened, Redfield learned that Captain Kidd had been hanged. He was sad about his friend's death. But Captain Kidd's treasure belonged to him now!

Part III

MORE PIRATE STUFF

Pirate Quiz

Take this quiz to see what you know about piracy.

1. There were two types of pirate ships. True or false?

2. The Golden Age of Piracy was during the nineteenth and twentieth centuries. True or false?

3. One of the greatest pirates was Captain Jack Sparrow. True or false?

4. Port Royal, Jamaica, was a favorite pirate hangout during the 1600s. True or false?

5. Edward Teach got the nickname "Blackbeard" because he always wore black clothes. True or false?

6. There were many officers aboard a pirate ship. Each officer had different responsibilities. What officer was the captain's second in command, and what were some of his duties?

7. Scurvy was a problem for pirates. True or false?

8. Pirates had a Code of Conduct. True or false?

9. Lots of people came to see pirates hanged. The largest crowd at a pirate execution was for the hanging of Stede Bonnet. True or false?

10. What pirate captured one of the biggest treasures but died poor?

11. Pirates painted over their gun ports to hide them. True or false?

12. What is "careening"?

13. Did pirates really walk around with parrots on their shoulders?

14. What kind of treasure did pirates like to get?

15. Did pirates usually bury treasure?

16. The most popular name for a pirate ship was *Adventure*. True or false?

17. Did some pirates have wooden legs?

18. Which pirate served as Captain Charles Vane's first mate and later took command of his ship?

19. There were four types of pirate flags. True or false?

20. Were there any female pirates?

21. What did pirates eat?

22. Did pirates have long lives and die of old age?

23. When a pirate was marooned, he was left on an island with nothing but the clothes on his back. True or false?

24. What was the usual punishment for mutiny?

25. Piracy is still taking place today. True or false?

Pirate Activities

1. What would your pirate Code of Conduct be? Write a Code of Conduct that you would enforce if you were a pirate captain. You can use the Code of Conduct found on page 46 as a guide.

2. Assemble a crew. Choose classmates and assign them roles. You would be the captain, of course. What other crew members would you need? Hint: This information is given somewhere in this book.

3. Make a poster showing the life of a pirate. It can be pictures cut out of magazines or newspapers, hand drawings, stickers, or whatever you like. Some suggestions: a sailing ship, parrot, spyglass, weapons, treasure, and common pirate food.

4. Write a one-page essay describing who your favorite pirate was and why.

5. Take an online tour and learn more about piracy at www.pirates-of-nassau.com. What did you learn? Do you want to be a pirate? Why or why not?

6. Write a pirate story. Pretend that you wake up and find yourself on a pirate ship in the 1700s. What happens next? Are you getting ready for battle? Are you looking for a merchant ship? Are you being chased by the navy? Did you come aboard on your own or were you forced into piracy?

   Or you can make up your own story, such as what if you are vacationing with your family and best friend on Sullivan's Island when you find a map showing buried pirate treasure. You and your friend decide to try to find the treasure but decide to tell no one, not even your family, what you are up to. What happens next?

7. You might think pirates don't exist anymore. Wrong! Piracy is an even bigger problem in some parts of the world today than it was in earlier times. Write or talk about how we fight piracy today. What weapons do pirates use today? How do we combat them? Do you think that piracy will ever end?

Pirate Museums

There are many great maritime museums. Maritime means the museum has exhibits about the sea. Most maritime museums have pirate displays. Check www.maritimemuseums.net to find museums and more.

North Carolina Maritime Museum

315 Front Street
Beaufort, NC 28516
(252) 728-7317
 www.ncmaritime.org
This museum highlights North Carolina maritime history, including the life of Blackbeard and the ongoing excavation of his flagship, and offers several summer programs for kids.

Graveyard of the Atlantic Museum

Hatteras-Ocracoke Ferry Terminal and U.S. Coast Guard Base
59200 Museum Drive
Hatteras Island, NC 27943
(252) 986-2995
www.graveyardoftheatlantic.com
The Outer Banks has been nicknamed the "Graveyard of the Atlantic" because of all the shipwrecks that have happened in the area. This museum has shipwreck exhibits and artifacts and much more.

On the Water: Stories from Maritime America
National Museum of American History

Smithsonian Institution
Washington, DC 20560
(202) 357-2025
http://americanhistory.si.edu/
This is an 8,000-foot permanent exhibit showing U.S. maritime history.

New England Pirate Museum

274 Derby Street
Salem, MA 01970
(978) 741-2800
www.piratemuseum.org
Here you can board a pirate ship, explore a cave, see pirate treasure, and much more.

The Pirates of Nassau Museum

At the waterfront near the Strawmarket (downtown at King and George Streets)
Nassau, Bahamas
(242) 356-3759
www.pirates-of-nassau.com
See pirate artifacts, buccaneer exhibits, and treasure; go aboard a pirate ship; and much more.

Pirate Soul Museum

524 Front Street
Key West, FL 33040
(305) 292-1113
www.piratesoul.com
This museum is more than 5,000 square feet! It has almost 500 pirate artifacts on display in many exhibits.

Pirate Resources

Many good books have been written on piracy. Here are a few I think you'll enjoy:

Fiction

Barrie, J. M. *Peter Pan* (100th Anniversary Edition). Illustrated by Michael Hague. Henry Holt and Company, 2003.

Berry, Connie Lee. *Pirates in Paradise*. Kid's Fun Press, 2007.

Eaton, Cathy. *Curse of the Pirate's Treasure*. AuthorHouse, 2002.

Girone, John. *Under The Eagle's Beak: The Search for the Treasure of Pirate's Pit*. BookSurge Publishing, 2006.

Hope, B. T. *The Curse of the Bone Pirates: Nui Island Eco-Logical Adventures*. Nui Media & Entertainment, 2008.

Kidd, Rob. *Pirates of the Caribbean: Jack Sparrow #4: The Sword of Cortes*. Illustrated by Disney. Disney Press, 2006.

    Author's Note: This is part of a series of Jack Sparrow books.

Marsh, Carole. *The Mystery of Blackbeard the Pirate*. Galllopade International/Carole Marsh Books, 2003.

Pyle, Howard. *The Book of Pirates*. Dover Publications, 2000.

Stevenson, Robert Louis. *Treasure Island: A Young Reader's Edition of the Classic Adventure*. Illustrated by N.C. Wyeth. Courage Books (Running Press), 2002.

Wechter, Nell Wise. *Teach's Light: A Tale of Blackbeard the Pirate*. University of North Carolina Press, 1999.

Zucker, Jonny. *Cut-Throat Pirates*, Illustrated by Pete Smith. Stone Arch Books, 2007.

Nonfiction

Jones, Rob Lloyd, and Jörg Mühle. *See Inside Pirate Ships*. E.D.C. Publishing, 2007.

O'Donnell, Liam. *Pirate Treasure: Stolen Riches*. Capstone Press, 2006.

Tessaro, Chuck, and Anatoly Slepkov. *Big Book of Pirates*. Running Press, 2004.

Yolen, Jane. *Sea Queens: Women Pirates Around the World*. Illustrated by Christine Joy Pratt. Charlesbridge Publishing, 2008.

Activity Books

Monsen, Avery, and Jory John. *Pirate's Log: A Handbook for Aspiring Swashbucklers*. Illustrated by Gilbert Ford. Chronicle Books, 2008.

Robins, Deri, and George Buchanan. *The Great Pirate Activity Book*. Kingfisher, 1995.

Quiz Answers

1. False. There are many types of ships. This book discusses three of the most popular ships of the Golden Age of Piracy: the sloop, schooner, and brigantine. But there were also lots of others, like the galley, brig, galleon, and junk.

2. False. The period known as the Golden Age of Piracy was between the late seventeenth and early eighteenth centuries.

3. False. Captain Jack Sparrow is not mentioned in this book because he was not a real pirate. He is a character created for Disney's *Pirates of the Caribbean* movies.

4. True. Port Royal had few laws. Sailors, slave traders, gamblers, and pirates loved to hang out here. An earthquake destroyed this pirate paradise on June 7, 1692.

5. False. Blackbeard, also called the "Black-faced Devil" and "Fury from Hell," got his nickname because he had wild black hair and a long, thick black beard.

6. The quartermaster was second in command. He had many important jobs. He gave each man his share of what they stole from other ships. He punished crew members when needed and was also in charge of prisoners. The quartermaster also let the captain know when the crew was unhappy about anything.

7. True. In the mid-1750s, we found out that eating fresh fruit and vegetables could keep us from getting sick. Scurvy is a disease that comes from not eating enough fruits and vegetables. So, pirates added a lemon wedge or lime slice to their rum and ale!

8. True. There were rules of piracy. Black Bart's code is on page 46. In general, fighting was not allowed on a pirate ship. If any of the crew members had an argument, they had to take it off the ship. Another general rule said that a pirate had to be paid if he got injured in battle. He got paid more if he lost an eye rather than an arm.

9. False. The biggest crowd for a pirate execution was for **Captain Kidd**. His body was tarred so it would not rot as fast. Then it was put in a gibbet (cage). This was done so that no one could steal the body. Family and friends who wanted to give the pirate a burial might take the body if it was not locked in a steel cage. Pirates were hung in gibbets to show everyone what happened to pirates. After you saw a pirate like that, you might think twice about becoming a pirate yourself!

10. Henry "Long Ben" Avery. He captured millions of dollars in treasure but lost it all.

11. True. This was done at times to fool merchant ships. Pirates wanted the merchant ships to sail close enough for them to attack. Only pirate ships had lots of cannons on board. Merchant ships would not come near a pirate ship. So the only way to get them to come near was to hide the cannon ports by painting over them!

12. Careening means taking a ship out of the water to be cleaned. Then it was turned on its side. The ship's bottom was scraped to take off barnacles and worms. The crew members also repaired any damage that may have been done during a battle or while at sea. Pirates needed safe places to

do these jobs. They were easy to capture while their ship was on land for repairs and cleaning.

13. Yes! Parrots were popular with pirates. They made fun and easy pets. Parrots were worth a lot of money in London bird markets. Parrots made good gifts too.

14. Spanish gold doubloons (one doubloon was worth seven weeks' pay for a pirate crew, on average), pieces of eight (old Spanish pesos), weapons of any kind, gunpowder, all types of medicine, alcoholic beverages, gold or copper snuffboxes, fine fabrics (such as silk and linen), food (the best kinds were meat, sugar, and flour), jewelry, or anything that could be sold or traded.

15. No! Pirates did not worry about the future. They lived for the present. Most died in battle or from battle wounds or illness. Pirates only buried their treasure if they were afraid they might be caught. If the Royal Navy was after them, the pirates might hide the loot. They would not want to be caught with it on their ship because then the navy would know they were pirates. Captain Kidd hid his treasure. He tried to use it to make a deal with the authorities.

16. True. *Adventure* was the most commonly used name for a pirate ship. *Revenge* and *Fortune* were also popular names.

17. Yes! Pirates often got injured during battle or in shipboard accidents. If the pirate had a wounded leg that could not be healed or might get infected, it was cut off. A wooden leg replaced it. If a hand had to be cut off, a hook was used.

18. John "Calico Jack" Rackham. When first mate Rackham and the other crew members disagreed how Vane was running things, they mutinied and elected Rackham as their new leader. Rackham put Vane and some of his loyal men into a schooner. He let them sail away. That is how Calico Jack became captain of his first ship.

19. False. There were two types of pirate flags. One was a red flag (called a "Red Jack"). It was a warning to surrender so that no one would be harmed. The other type of flag was a black flag ("Jolly Roger"). The word "roger" means rogue or rover. The Jolly Roger flag meant that the victims would all die if they did not surrender. The pictures on the flags were personalized. This meant they were symbols of each pirate captain. The designs often had crossed bones, skulls, skeletons, and cutlasses.

20. Yes, though male pirates were far more common. Two female pirates are discussed in this book: Anne Bonny and Mary Read.

21. Anything they could get their hands on! The most popular pirate foods were turtles, turtle eggs, fish, wild boar and pig, birds, hens, hen eggs, hardtack (biscuits made of flour and water), and soup or stew. Wine, rum, and ale were popular drinks.

22. Not usually! One out of three pirates never made it back from sea. They often died from battle wounds or disease. There was not enough medicine to treat wounds and disease.

23. True. But this did not happen often. Marooning was up to the pirate captain. Some captains gave the pirate a tiny portion of food and water. They usually either left the pirate on a deserted island or set the pirate adrift in a rowboat.

24. Mutinous crew members were usually marooned as punishment.

25. True. Privateering lasted more than five thousand years. It came to an end in the early nineteenth century. That is when most countries signed an agreement that privateers would no longer be allowed. The end of privateering helped end most piracy. Improvements to shipbuilding and the military also helped end piracy. Or did it? Piracy is actually still a big problem today.

Scoring

19 out of 25 correct answers = You are ready to be a captain.

11 – 18 correct answers = You show promise, but you spend too much time partying in Jamaica!

5 –10 correct answers =We may have to put you on a desert island, matey!

0 – 4 correct answers = Not even Blackbeard could make you a pirate!

Index

Adventure, 11, 22, 26, 28, 29
Adventure Galley, 55, 58
Adventure Prize, 59
Arabian Coast, 41
Avery, Henry "Long Ben," 10, 41–42

Bahamas (*see also* New Providence),
    5, 21, 22, 31, 33, 35, 39, 42, 45, 51
Banister, Captain, 43
Barbados, 47, 51, 55
Bath, 26, 30
Beal, Captain, 45
Beaufort Inlet (*see* Topsail Inlet), 24,
    48
Bellomont, Lord, 55, 59, 60
Bermuda, 26
Black Bart (*see* Roberts, Bartholomew
    "Black Bart")
Blackbeard (*see* Teach, Edward
    "Blackbeard")
Blockade of Charleston, 24–25, 47
Bonnet, Stede "the Gentleman Pirate,"
    5, 22, 26, 47–50
Bonny, Anne, 5, 31–33, 35, 36, 37, 39
Boston Harbor, 43
Brisbau, Max, 61
Bristol, 21, 42
British Royal Navy, 5, 25, 26, 27, 28,
    35, 36, 43, 55, 57

Calico Jack (*see* Rackham, John
    "Calico Jack")
captain, 6, 7, 17, 19, 22, 30, 35, 41, 43,
    46, 53, 54, 55, 61
Caribbean Sea, 5, 7, 12, 16, 21, 22,
    55, 59
Carolinas, 10, 29, 41, 47, 48, 60
Charles Town (*see also* Charleston), 25
Charleston, 25, 25, 31, 33, 47, 48, 50,
    53, 59, 60, 61
Conception Bay, 45
Concorde, 21, 24
Crowley, 25
Cuba, 5, 22, 43
Curlew, 35

Deane, Tom, 39
Dominican Republic (*see also*
    Hispaniola), 22
Duke, 41

Eden, Governor, 25, 26
Edisto River, 53
England, 5, 21, 35, 41, 42, 48, 55, 57,
    58, 59
English Channel, 57
Execution Dock, 60

Fancy, 41, 42
France, 5, 26, 55

Gallows Point, 36, 54
Gang-i-Sawai, 41
Gardiners Island, 60
"Gold Bug, The," 59
Golden Age of Piracy, 5, 10
Gordon, Captain, 27, 28
Great Mogul, 41, 42, 58
Gulf of Aden, 41

Hands, Israel, 22, 29
Henry, 48
Herman, 45
Herriot, David, 50
Hispaniola, 5, 22, 39, 51
Holford, Captain, 53, 54
Hornigold, Benjamin, 21, 24

India, 42, 58
Indies, 39
International Maritime Bureau, 19
Ireland, 31, 42

Jamaica, 5, 33, 35, 36, 39, 43, 53, 54
Jane, 27
Java Sea, 19
Johnson, South Carolina Governor, 25,
    48, 50, 53

Kidd, William, 5, 10, 55–61
King William's War, 55
Knight, Tobias, 26, 27, 29

Lewis, William "Billy," 43–46
Lightfoot, Mr., 41
Livingston, Robert, 55
London, 59, 60
Long Ben (*see* Avery, Henry "Long
    Ben")

Madagascar, 5, 41, 57
Malabar, 57
Massachusetts Bay, 59
Maynard, Lieutenant, 27, 28, 29
McCaffrey, Darby, 43, 45
Money Island, 60
Moore, William, 57, 60
Morning Star, 43

New Providence (*see also* Bahamas),
    5, 31, 35, 51
Newfoundland, 41, 45
Newgate Prison, 60
North Carolina, 24, 25, 26, 29, 30, 35,
    41, 51, 60

Ocracoke Island, 26, 27, 29, 53
Odel, Samuel, 29
Ormond, Mary, 26, 30

pirates (*see individual entries*)
    modern-day, 19
Poe, Edgar Allan, 59

Point Negril, 33
Port Royal, 33, 36, 43, 53, 54
privateers (*see individual entries*)
Protestant Caesar, 22, 24

Quedagh Merchant, 58
Queen Anne's Revenge, 21, 22, 24, 26,
    48
Queen Anne's War, 5, 21, 24

Rackham, John "Calico Jack," 31, 33,
    35–36, 39, 53
Ranger, 27, 28
Read, Mary, 33, 36, 37–39
Red Sea, 41, 57
Redfield, John, 61
Revenge, 22, 26, 47
Rhett, Colonel William, 48, 50, 53
Richard, Lieutenant, 22
Roberts, Bartholomew "Black Bart,"
    46
Rogers, Governor Woodes, 33, 39, 45,
    51
Royal James, 48
Royal Navy (*see* British Royal Navy)

Sea Nymph, 48
ships (*see individual entries*)
shipwreck, 24
Snow, Edward Rowe, 30
South Carolina, 24, 25, 31, 35, 41, 43,
    45, 48, 53, 59, 60
South China Sea, 19
Spain, 35
Spotswood, Virginia Governor, 25, 26,
    27, 29
Stone Prison, 59
Sullivan's Island, 59, 60

Teach, Edward "Blackbeard," 19,
    21–30, 47, 48, 53
Teach's Hole, 27, 29
Thames River, 60
Thatch, Edward (*see* Teach, Edward
    "Blackbeard")
Topsail Inlet, 24, 26, 48
treasure, 6, 7, 10, 13, 18, 21, 25, 29,
    51, 59, 60, 61
Trott, Bahamas Governor, 42
Trott, Justice, 50
Tucker, Captain, 43

Vane, Charles, 10, 35, 51–54

West Indies, 35, 37, 41
Whedbee, Judge Charles H., 30
White Point, 50
Wragg, Samuel, 25

Yeates, 51, 53

Here are some other books from Pineapple Press on related topics. For a complete catalog, visit our website at www.pineapplepress.com. Or write to Pineapple Press, P.O. Box 3889, Sarasota, Florida 34230-3889, or call (800) 746-3275.

Also By Terrance Zepke

Lighthouses of the Carolinas for Kids by Terrance Zepke. The history of and facts about lighthouses along the Carolina coasts. Includes color photos and illustrations, ghost stories, and a quiz. Ages 9 and up. (pb)

Pirates of the Carolinas, 2nd Edition by Terrance Zepke. Thirteen of the most fascinating buccaneers in the history of piracy, including Henry Avery, Blackbeard, Anne Bonny, Captain Kidd, Calico Jack, and Stede Bonnet. (pb)

Best Ghost Tales of North Carolina, 2nd Edition, and *Best Ghost Tales of South Carolina* by Terrance Zepke. The actors of the Carolinas' past linger among the living in these thrilling collections of ghost tales. Use Zepke's tips to conduct your own ghost hunt. (pb)

Ghosts of the Carolina Coasts by Terrance Zepke. Thirty-two ghost stories from the coasts of the Carolinas that will make your hair stand on end. (pb)

Ghosts and Legends of the Carolina Coasts by Terrance Zepke. More spine-chilling tales and fascinating legends from the coastal regions of North and South Carolina. (pb)

For more information on Terrance Zepke's books and future projects, check out www.terrancezepke.com.

Other Pineapple Press Titles

Twenty Florida Pirates by Kevin M. McCarthy, with paintings by William L. Trotter. Introduces twenty of the most notorious Florida pirates, from the English privateers of the 1500s to present-day smugglers and "yachtjackers." Meet Sir Francis Drake, Black Caesar, Blackbeard, Jean Lafitte, and José Gaspar. (pb)

Florida Lighthouses for Kids by Elinor De Wire. Learn about the people who designed and built Florida's lighthouses, meet some of the keepers, see how lighthouses operate, find out about their new roles as museums, and more. Ages 9 and up. (pb)

The Legend of the Lowcountry Liar and Other Tales of a Tall Order by Brian McCréight. Thirteen tall tales told by Jim Aisle, the Lowcountry Liar himself, whose homespun yarns weave fact and fiction like Gullah women make sweetgrass baskets. (pb)